CW00502424

Danny Cipriani

Danny Cipriani is indeed an English professional rugby union player known for his versatility in playing both as a fly-half and a fullback. As of my last knowledge update in September 2021, he had a career that included stints with several notable rugby clubs and the England national team:

Early Career: Danny Cipriani began his rugby career in the Wasps academy in 2003. He made his senior debut for Wasps in 2006.

Club Career:

Wasps: Cipriani played for London Wasps from 2006 to 2010, making a significant impact in the Premiership.
Melbourne Rebels: He briefly played for the Melbourne Rebels in Super Rugby during the 2011 season.
Sale Sharks: Cipriani joined Sale Sharks in 2012 and played there until 2016.
Gloucester: He then moved to Gloucester Rugby and played for the club from 2018 to 2020.
Bath: Cipriani played for Bath Rugby in the Premiership, most recently up to my last knowledge update in September 2021.
International Career: Danny Cipriani earned 16 caps for the England national rugby team. His international career had its ups and downs, with periods of selection and omission from the national squad.

Notable Achievements: Throughout his career, Cipriani was recognized for his skill and ability to control a rugby match. He gained a reputation as a talented and creative playmaker.

Early career

Schooling and Scholarships: Danny Cipriani attended Wimbledon College prep school in London, Donhead. Recognized as a rugby talent during his time there, he received a full scholarship. To further his rugby development, he was advised to move to the Junior House of The Oratory School near Reading. Later, he transferred to Whitgift School in Croydon after Common Entrance.

Multi-Sport Athlete: Cipriani was not limited to rugby alone. He was a versatile and accomplished athlete:

He played junior football for Queens Park Rangers and received youth terms from Reading Football Club.

Cipriani also participated in schoolboy cricket for Berkshire and Oxfordshire, even receiving an invitation to join Surrey County Cricket Club as a batsman.

He played squash at the county level, showcasing his athletic prowess in multiple sports.

Introduction to Rugby: Danny Cipriani's early exposure to rugby came when he played for Rosslyn Park in Roehampton, where he developed a passion for the game. His precocious talent and flamboyant playing style were encouraged by youth level coaches. He also received support and mentorship from figures like Bobby Walsh, a local hero who took a special interest in his development at the club.

Rugby Development: Danny Cipriani's talent and dedication to rugby continued to shine as he progressed through his school years. His move to Whitgift School in Croydon likely provided him with valuable opportunities to hone his rugby skills further. The mentorship of coaches and the guidance of local heroes like Bobby Walsh played a crucial role in shaping his playing style and passion for the game.

Professional Rugby Career: After his early development in school and club rugby, Cipriani's skills and potential were evident to professional rugby scouts. He made his debut for London Wasps in 2006, marking the beginning of his professional rugby career. His time at Wasps was marked by impressive performances, and he quickly gained recognition as a rising star in English rugby.

Versatility and Style: One of Danny Cipriani's notable traits was his flair and creativity on the rugby field. He was known for his ability to read the game, make dynamic plays, and execute skillful kicks. His versatility, being equally adept as a fly-half and fullback, made him a valuable asset to his teams.

International Experience: Cipriani's talent earned him caps for the England national rugby team. Representing his country at the international level was a significant achievement in his career, though it was marked by periods of both success and challenges.

Life Beyond Rugby: Beyond his sporting achievements, Danny Cipriani has been a figure of interest off the field as well. He's known for his outspoken personality, involvement in social causes, and engagement with media and entertainment.

Ongoing Journey: As of my last knowledge update in September 2021, Cipriani's career was marked by club transfers and continued dedication to the sport of rugby. His journey in professional rugby and life beyond the sport was a subject of interest to fans and followers.

Challenges and Triumphs: Like many professional athletes, Danny Cipriani faced his share of challenges and triumphs throughout his career. Injuries, competition for positions, and periods of being out of favor with national team selectors were part of his journey. However, he also experienced moments of glory, contributing to memorable victories for his club and country.

Club Loyalty: Despite moving between different clubs during his career, Cipriani's loyalty to the game of rugby remained constant. His passion for the sport and dedication to improving his skills were evident in his performances on the field. He often spoke about his love for the game and the importance of hard work and resilience.

Off-Field Impact: Danny Cipriani's influence extended beyond rugby. He used his platform to advocate for various causes, including mental health awareness and social justice issues. His candid and open approach to discussing personal challenges, including mental health struggles, resonated with many, and he became a vocal advocate for breaking stigmas associated with mental health.

Media Presence: Cipriani's presence in the media was notable. He engaged with fans and followers through social media and was known for sharing insights into his life, interests, and thoughts. This openness allowed fans to connect with him on a more personal level.

Legacy: While Danny Cipriani's playing career had its ebbs and flows, he undoubtedly left a mark on the rugby world. His creativity, skill, and versatility made him a unique talent, and his willingness to speak out on important issues endeared him to many beyond the rugby community.

Future Endeavors: Beyond his playing days, Cipriani's future endeavors remained of interest to his fans and the public. Whether in coaching, media, or other ventures, there was anticipation about what he might pursue next

Club career

Wasps

Early Days at Wasps: Danny Cipriani's journey with Wasps began when he joined their academy in 2003. He made his senior debut for the club against Bristol in the Powergen Cup in December 2004 at the age of 17. Over the following years, he continued to develop his skills within the Wasps setup.

Rise to Prominence: In the 2006–07 season, Cipriani joined the Wasps Academy full-time and played for the under-21 team and Wasps A team before making more regular appearances for the first team in 2007. He played a significant role as Wasps won the 2007 Heineken Cup Final.

Taking the Fly-Half Role: After Alex King's departure from Wasps in the summer of 2007, the fly-half position became vacant, and Cipriani was given the opportunity to play in that crucial role. His performances earned him recognition, and he quickly established himself as a key figure in the team.

Injury Setbacks: Cipriani's promising career at Wasps was marred by injury setbacks. In May 2008, he suffered a serious fracture dislocation of his right ankle during a semi-final play-off victory over Bath. This injury not only ruled him out of England's tour but also prevented him from participating in Wasps' victory in the 2007–08 Premiership final.

Remarkable Recovery: Despite the severity of his ankle injury, Cipriani made a remarkable recovery and returned to the field ahead of schedule. His determination and work ethic during his recovery were praised by his sprint coach, Margot Wells.

International Return and Scrutiny: Following his recovery, Cipriani regained the England number 10 shirt for the 2008 Autumn Internationals. However, he faced criticism after two poor performances in defeats to South Africa and Australia. There were also discussions about his high-profile relationship with model Kelly Brook and concerns about his commitment to rugby.

Ongoing Challenges: Cipriani's career at Wasps continued to be marked by injury challenges. Despite enjoying strong performances in the 2009–10 season, he suffered another injury, ruling him out of the Autumn Internationals for England.

Farewell to Wasps: Cipriani played his last home match for London Wasps on 1 May 2010 against Cardiff Blues in the Amlin Challenge Cup semi-final. His time at Wasps was characterized by highs and lows, showcasing his talent and determination in the face of adversity.

Move to Other Clubs: After his tenure with Wasps, Danny Cipriani's career took him to several other clubs in the Premiership and Super Rugby, each chapter adding new experiences and challenges.

Melbourne Rebels: Following his time with Wasps, Cipriani ventured to Super Rugby, signing with the Melbourne Rebels in Australia. His move to the Southern Hemisphere was a significant step in his career, showcasing his ambition to play at the highest level of the sport.

Return to the Premiership: After his stint in Australia, Cipriani returned to the Premiership and joined Sale Sharks. His time with Sale Sharks saw him continue to display his playmaking abilities and influence on the field.

Gloucester: Cipriani later moved to Gloucester Rugby, where he continued to be a prominent figure in English rugby. His performances at Gloucester further solidified his reputation as a skilled and versatile player.

Bath: His journey in the Premiership continued as he joined Bath Rugby. Playing for Bath, Cipriani continued to be a valuable asset to his team, contributing with his tactical awareness and ability to create scoring opportunities.

England Caps: Throughout his club career, Cipriani's performances occasionally earned him call-ups to the England national team. His time representing England at the international level was marked by moments of brilliance, showcasing his ability to control matches and create scoring opportunities.

Off-Field Endeavors: In addition to his rugby career, Cipriani's off-field endeavors garnered attention. His outspoken personality, advocacy for mental health awareness, and engagement with social and cultural issues made him a prominent figure beyond the rugby pitch.

Legacy and Future: As of my last knowledge update in September 2021, Danny Cipriani's career was still ongoing, and there was anticipation about his future endeavors, both in rugby and in his personal life. His journey was a testament to his dedication to the sport, his versatility, and his determination to overcome challenges.

Melbourne Rebels

Move to Melbourne Rebels: In February 2010, it was announced that Danny Cipriani would join the Melbourne Rebels in Super Rugby. His move to the Australian club generated significant interest and speculation, particularly regarding his chances of being selected for the England national team in the 2011 Rugby World Cup.

Training with Football Clubs: Ahead of his move to Melbourne, Cipriani engaged in training sessions with football clubs in London. He trained with Queens Park Rangers and Tottenham Hotspur, exploring opportunities in football while preparing for his rugby venture. His diverse athletic background allowed him to adapt to different training environments.

Training in the United States: Cipriani also traveled to the United States, specifically Denver, for what he referred to as "altitude training." This demonstrated his commitment to physical conditioning and improving his rugby skills.

Training with Milton Keynes Dons: In addition to his football training, Cipriani spent time with the Milton Keynes Dons, a football club, and was reportedly offered a chance to sign with them if his experience in Melbourne did not go as planned.

Challenges and Contributions: Despite issues with his Australian work visa, Cipriani joined the Melbourne Rebels for pre-season training in late 2010. He primarily trained as a fly-half and was even named one of two captains for friendly trials against the Tongans.

On-Field Performances: Cipriani's time with the Rebels saw him making valuable contributions on the field. In one of the Rebels' early Super Rugby games against the Brumbies, he not only scored the team's first points with a penalty kick but also played a pivotal role in securing the team's first-ever win.

Off-Field Challenges: Cipriani's time with the Rebels was not without off-field challenges. There were instances of ill-discipline, including an incident where he was accused of taking a bottle of vodka from a Melbourne bar. These issues led to fines and even being stood down from matches.

Defensive Criticism: During the 2011 season, Cipriani faced criticism for his defensive skills. Rugby pundits and observers noted areas where he needed improvement, which is a common aspect of player development in professional sports.

Challenges in Melbourne: Despite his talent and contributions on the field, Cipriani's tenure with the Melbourne Rebels was marked by ups and downs. His ill-discipline off the field, as well as defensive issues on it, brought about challenges and scrutiny.

Off-Field Conduct: Cipriani's off-field conduct, including the incident involving the alleged taking of a bottle of vodka, raised concerns within the club and led to disciplinary actions. The club's standards and expectations of its players were made clear, and Cipriani faced consequences for his actions.

Contributions and Promise: On a more positive note, Cipriani's performances on the field showed promise. He demonstrated his playmaking abilities and his ability to score points for the Rebels, contributing significantly to the team's efforts.

Moving Forward: After his time with the Melbourne Rebels, Danny Cipriani's career trajectory continued with moves to other clubs. His experiences in Super Rugby and the Premiership had given him valuable exposure to different styles of play and a diverse range of teammates.

Personal Growth and Development: Cipriani's journey in rugby was not just about his on-field performances but also about personal growth and development. He faced challenges, learned from them, and continued to evolve as a player and as an individual.

Impact on English Rugby: While his time with the Melbourne Rebels might not have led to a prolonged stint in Australia, Cipriani's move made him one of the few English players to venture into Super Rugby. This experience likely contributed to his overall growth as a rugby player and may have influenced his approach to the game upon returning to England.

Legacy and Beyond: Danny Cipriani's career was marked by its diversity, including experiences in different leagues and countries. As of my last knowledge update in September 2021, he had continued his rugby journey, making moves to other clubs. His legacy extended beyond the field, as he remained a vocal advocate for various causes and engaged with fans and followers through his media presence.

Return to Premiership

Return to Sale Sharks: After his stint in Australia with the Melbourne Rebels, Danny Cipriani returned to the Premiership by signing a new three-year contract with Sale Sharks ahead of the 2013–14 season. His return to the Premiership was marked by impressive performances, including scoring over 200 points and helping Sale reach the LV= Cup Final. His contributions played a crucial role in Sale Sharks' survival bid in the Aviva Premiership.

International Selection: Cipriani's performances with Sale Sharks didn't go unnoticed, as he was selected for England's 30-man squad for the three-match tour to New Zealand in June 2014, marking his return to the international stage.

Rejoining Wasps: In February 2016, it was announced that Cipriani would once again rejoin the Wasps for the 2016–17 season. His return to Wasps saw him reunite with the club where he began his professional career and contributed to their efforts in the Premiership.

Move to Gloucester Rugby: After his second stint with Wasps, Cipriani made another club move, this time to Gloucester Rugby for the 2018–19 season. His time with Gloucester was marked by strong performances, earning him recognition and accolades within the rugby community.

Player of the Year: In May 2019, Danny Cipriani was honored by the Rugby Players Association as the Player of the Year, a testament to his consistent and outstanding performances during that season.

Departure from Gloucester: On 15 December 2020, it was announced that Cipriani had left Gloucester, marking the end of his tenure with the club.

Joining Bath Rugby: In March 2021, Danny Cipriani signed a one-year deal with Bath Rugby ahead of the 2021–22 season, officially joining the club in early May 2021. His move to Bath represented another chapter in his career as he continued to contribute his skills and experience to Premiership rugby.

International career

Early International Experience: Danny Cipriani's international journey began at a young age when he captained the England under-16 team. He continued to progress through the ranks and played fly-half for the England under-19 side in the Under-19 World Cup, although his participation was cut short due to a head injury.

Saxons and Near-Miss for 2007 Rugby World Cup: Cipriani was part of the England Saxons' side that won the Churchill Cup at Twickenham in 2007. Despite spending the summer in the England senior squad's training camp, he narrowly missed out on selection for the 2007 Rugby World Cup.

Debut and "Inappropriate Behavior" Incident: Cipriani's senior England debut was highly anticipated. His starting debut was scheduled for a match against Scotland in the 2008 Six Nations Championship. However, just days before the match, he was axed from the squad due to what was described as "inappropriate behavior." This incident involved him leaving a London nightclub late at night.

Debut Against Ireland: Despite the setback, Cipriani made his England debut against Ireland on 15 March 2008. He replaced Jonny Wilkinson at fly-half and had an impressive match, converting all his goal kicks and contributing to a 33–10 victory for England.

Return to International Rugby: After a period of absence from the international scene, Cipriani made his return to the England squad for the 2014 England rugby union tour of New Zealand. He came off the bench in the 1st and 3rd tests of the tour.

2015 Six Nations and Try Against Italy: Cipriani was named on the bench for the opening match against Wales in the 2015 Six Nations but did not make an appearance. However, in the following match against Italy, he replaced George Ford during the second half and made an immediate impact by scoring a try with his second touch. England won that match 47–17.

Exclusion from 2015 Rugby World Cup: Despite his contributions, Cipriani was ultimately left out of the final 31-man squad for the 2015 Rugby World Cup, a significant disappointment given his earlier promise in the England setup.

Exclusion from Eddie Jones' Squad: In 2016, under the new coaching regime of Eddie Jones, Cipriani was left out of the elite player squad for the Six Nations, signaling a new phase in his international career.

Opposing Team: Pacific Islanders

Location: London, England
Venue: Twickenham Stadium
Competition: 2008 Autumn Internationals
Date: 8 November 2008
Result: Win
Score: 39 – 13
Opposing Team: Italy

Location: London, England
Venue: Twickenham Stadium
Competition: 2015 Six Nations
Date: 14 February 2015
Result: Win
Score: 47 – 17
Opposing Team: France

Location: Paris, France
Venue: Stade de France
Competition: 2015 Rugby World Cup Warm-Up
Date: 22 August 2015
Result: Loss
Score: 20 – 25

Danny Cipriani's career has not been without its share of controversies. Here are some notable incidents:

Drunk-Driving Conviction (2015): On 1 June 2015, Cipriani was arrested for drunk-driving after the car he was driving collided with a taxi at 05:15. Following a five-day trial, he was convicted of drunk-driving before Westminster Magistrates' Court on 24 June 2016. He was ordered to pay a total of £7,620 in fines and costs and banned from driving for 18 months.

Arrest in Jersey (2018): During a pre-season tour in Jersey on 15 August 2018, Cipriani was arrested after an incident at a nightclub in St Helier. He was charged with several offenses, including common assault on a doorman, larceny, assault on a police woman, resisting arrest, and being disorderly on licensed premises.

These controversies garnered significant media attention and affected Cipriani's public image. While he faced legal consequences for his actions, he also worked to rebuild his reputation both on and off the rugby field.

Personal life

Mixed Heritage: Danny Cipriani has a mixed racial background. His father is Afro-Trinidadian with distant Italian heritage, while his mother is English. Despite his parents' separation soon after his birth, he has maintained contact with his father.

Hospitalization in 2013: In 2013, Cipriani was hospitalized after being hit by a double-decker bus in Leeds. The incident occurred during an end-of-season night out with his Sale Sharks teammates, participating in a pub crawl known as the Otley Run. He suffered a concussion but was kept in the hospital overnight for x-rays. Fortunately, he was able to recover from the incident.

Advocacy for Animal Rights: In 2014, Cipriani posed shirtless for a PETA (People for the Ethical Treatment of Animals) "Ink Not Mink" advert. In the campaign, he showed off his tattoos to raise awareness for the anti-fur cause.

Relationship with Caroline Flack: In 2019, Cipriani dated television presenter Caroline Flack, which garnered attention in the media.

Marriage to Victoria: Cipriani is currently married to Victoria, although further details about their relationship are not provided.

Struggles with Depression: In February 2020, Cipriani revealed that he has been dealing with depression since the age of 22, shedding light on his mental health challenges and raising awareness about the issue.

Printed in Great Britain
by Amazon

33773992R00020